The Ethic:

Book of Revelation

Ian Paul

Managing Editor, Grove Books Ltd

Director of Partnership Development,
St John's College Nottingham

GROVE BOOKS LIMITED
RIDLEY HALL RD   CAMBRIDGE   CB3 9HU

Contents

1 Heart of Darkness? 3

2 A Many-Splendoured Thing 6

   An Ethic of Oppression 6

   An Ethic of Resistance and Justification 8

   An Ethic of Critical Engagement 10

   An Ethic of Suspicion and Crisis 11

3 Four Hot Potatoes... 14

   Gender 14

   Violence.. 17

   Heterophobia 20

   Politics 22

4 Metaphorical Ethics... 23

   Notes 27

The Cover Illustration is by Peter Ashton

Acknowledgements
Many thanks to the Grove Ethics group for enouragement, patience and trust, and to Greg
Forster in particular for comments on the text. Thanks too to my colleague Stephen Travis for
nuggets of information and to Dona and Susanne for being flexible. Thanks mostly to my wife,
Maggie, for patient affirmation, and to Elizabeth, Ben and Rebecca for passion for all things
revealed.

First Impression January 2005
ISSN 1470-854X
ISBN 1 85174 582 3

Heart of Darkness?

'Mistah Kurtz—he dead.'

The climax of Joseph Conrad's nineteenth-century novel *Heart of Darkness* comes with the death of the European explorer Kurtz, venturing to take his civilized outlook on life into the dark heart of the untamed continent of Africa. Francis Ford Coppola's twentieth-century cinematic remake of the story, the 1979 cult classic *Apocalypse Now*, saw Colonel Kurtz of the US Army similarly plunging, Western ideals in tow, into the dark heart of Vietnam, only to become disillusioned with his cultural inheritance and mesmerized by the total commitment of the Vietcong to their war of liberation.[1]

But the title of the film throws some light on why expounding the ethics of the Book of Revelation has been so problematic:

---

1 In the first place, the popular use of the terms 'apocalypse' and 'apocalyptic' has been collapsed into simply standing for some severe crisis that threatens the existence of whatever is perceived to constitute 'civilization.' In the case of *Apocalypse Now*, the alien cultural values of the native Vietnamese and the defeat of what was perceived to be the most powerful army in the world threatened American perception of their own invincibility and so their role within the Cold War world order. (The film was made within ten years of the iconic collapse of Saigon.) In other, more recent, celluloid apocalypses, the threat has come from meteorites, global warming or (more traditionally) aliens from another planet. But this rather one-dimensional use of language associated with the Book of Revelation has seeped into the church's consciousness, so that it is still possible to find commentators who regard Revelation simply as 'crisis literature.'[2]

> *This rather one-dimensional use of language associated with the Book of Revelation has seeped into the church's consciousness*

2 In the second place, there is a strong strand of popular and semi-popular theology which forms a powerful interpretative key to Revelation for many Christians, and which has over the years led to the popular flattening of apocalyptic understanding mentioned above. This theology is usually known as 'dispensational pre-millennialism' and its origins go back to J N Darby, the nineteenth-century disillusioned Anglican clergyman who was a founding leader of the Plymouth Brethren. After a period of seclusion, Darby started teaching his new theory in 1829, but it did not become widely known until it was published as part of the study notes in the Scofield Reference Bible in 1909.[3]

'Classical' pre-millennialism was probably the dominant view in the early church—most believed that the chronology of Revelation 19 and 20 should be taken at face value, so that Christ would return to earth and reign for a (literal) thousand years before Satan was released again for a short time before his final defeat and the descent of the New Jerusalem in Rev 21.[4] But Darby put this into a wider framework—the age of the church was the seventh and final 'dispensation' of the world, each dispensation having a distinctive challenge for humanity, who failed in a distinctive way and who could be saved by a distinctive act of God, in this dispensation the atoning death of Christ. And he added significant detail. By conflating a particular reading of Matthew 24.36 with 1 Thess 4.11 and the 'time, times and half a time' of Revelation 11 and 12, he argued that Christians would be 'raptured' away to be with the Lord, leaving the earth without Christian witness for a period of three-and-a-half years, which would be the period of intense 'tribulation.'[5]

From an ethical perspective this compresses Revelation's vision of discipleship into a single decision of whether or not to follow Christ

From an ethical perspective, this compresses Revelation's vision of discipleship into a single decision of whether or not to follow Christ. Since Revelation appears (in this reading) to be offering a complex but essentially repetitive challenge—make sure you are on the right side of the divide—there is no intermediate period of Christian living within which one must make ethical judgments. And, naturally, those proposing such a reading also believe that 'the end' is imminent, so Revelation's lack of vision for Christian living is matched by that of those calling for the crisis moment to be realized in the here and now.

3 In the third place, scholarly developments in the study of Revelation have by and large been kept well away from the popular Christian Bible-reading public. There is some irony in the fact that in the 1840s, at almost exactly the same time as J N Darby was first teaching his theory of the rapture, four German scholars, apparently independently, were proposing a new solution to the riddle of the mark of the beast, the 'human number' 666 of Revelation 13.18.[6] But this solution is (in my experience) almost completely unknown by church-going Christians and by most clergy. And to match this divide between scholarship and popular understandings, the mainline churches have resolutely avoided reading Revelation, virtually sidelining it in their lectionaries, for example, and so perpetuating the lack of contact between the academic and confessional use of the book.[7]

How then can we engage with the ethics of Revelation? Unlike with earlier booklets in this series looking at biblical ethics, it is not possible to refer to a widely supported reading of the text in question and make observations about the ethical shape of these agreed understandings. Instead, I will examine a few, widely differing readings of Revelation to highlight some of the connections between hermeneutical (interpretative) strategies and perceptions of Revelation's ethics. I will then examine some key ethical issues to see whether it is possible to sense a coherent perspective of the text on these issues, or at the least whether the text suggests some guidelines or boundaries on these issues. Finally, I will reflect on the distinctive contribution that Revelation makes to Christian ethical reflection; perhaps it is the case that we cannot talk of 'the ethics of Revelation' but can talk of the ethical imperative that Revelation offers across different contexts of reading.

2   A Many-Splendoured Thing

From a literary perspective, Revelation is an 'open' text for at least two reasons.

In the first place, it contains a mixture of genres of writing, and at times the change from one genre to another is quite rapid.[8] Since genre is the way in which the writer of a text communicates expectations to potential readers, these changes of genres lead to a sense of mixed expectations on the part of the reader, who then has to make an interpretative decision as to which set of expectations to prioritize. In the second place, some argue that the imagery (in literary terms, the metaphors) of Revelation is inherently open to a range of interpretations.

In part because of this openness, Revelation has given rise to a wide variety of interpretations, especially in the last two centuries. Looking at these different interpretations is like shining a light into the text from different angles; as we see how this light reflects and refracts, we can see more of the nature of the text, not least from an ethical perspective.

The four readings that I will look at in this chapter are a feminist political reading, an ethnic political reading from the context of South African Apartheid, a futurist dispensational reading, and an economic political reading from a Western perspective.[9] None of these is from a 'traditional' Western, devotional perspective; we learn more about the text by shining lights from very different angles.

Tina Pippin: an Ethic of Oppression

Tina Pippin brings to Revelation a thorough-going feminist ideology—that is, her feminism has not only personal and political but also philosophical and literary dimensions to it. So every aspect of engaging with a text like Revelation is affected by her ideological stance, and in *Death and Desire: the Rhetoric of Gender in the Apocalypse of John*[10] she subjects Revelation to what she calls an ideological critique. It feels at times as though the very fact that Revelation is a text, rather than something visual or oral, and that it has canonical status as part of an authoritative collection of Scriptures, are themselves problematic aspects of the book for her.

Though her work is described as 'innovative' she is certainly indebted to those who have gone before her, not least the feminist biblical scholars Adela Yarbro-Collins and Elisabeth Schüssler Fiorenza, both of whom have specialized in the study of Revelation and written significant commentaries on it. In fact, there are so many others cited in the book that at times it feels as much like a critique of philosophical literary theory as an analysis of the Book of Revelation.

Ideology and Ethics
Since Pippin's reading is ideological, it is also at every point an ethical reading, and Pippin acknowledges this explicitly at a number of points. Thus her ideological critique is expressed in (occasionally) positive or (predominantly) negative evaluations of Revelation's ethic, either as expressed within the text or as seen in its use in art or subsequent interpretation in the oppression of women and of 'outsiders.' Her book includes a selection of mediaeval and contemporary art, with comments highlighting the destructive nature of the imagery itself, or the way in which the imagery draws out the fundamentally oppressive nature of the text.

The summary of her view of Revelation comes fairly early on (p 47) and quite explicitly:

> I want to focus on the clearly identified women in the text who are destroyed and on the general 'apocalypse of women' brought about in the utopian vision of the New Jerusalem. By the 'apocalypse of women' I mean the misogyny and disenfranchisement that are at the roots of gender relations, accompanied by (hetero) sexism and racism, along with violence, poverty, disempowerment, and fear. Apocalypse is the re-veiling of women, the silencing and marginalization of women.

This criticism of Revelation's ethic starts from the very nature of the text, as one that is an 'oppositional text' (p 23), that is, it deals in the binary oppositions of good and evil, life and death that are in themselves unsatisfactory to Pippin's feminist ideological perspective. So, although there is in theory a positive message of political liberation, the expression of this liberation is unsatisfactory since 'one person's utopia may be another person's dystopia' (p 30). If, as Revelation appears to depict, the oppressors and oppressed simply change places, this is no vision of hope. Moreover, the route to the vision of the New Jerusalem is littered with male-controlled stereotypes of images of women, both good and evil, who are either passive or killed with glee all the while evoking suppressed male desire. And at the end, although those in the New Jerusalem are in theory of 'all nations, tribes and languages' this is not really an inclusive group, since 'there is no room for Jews or pagans or anyone who refuses to acknowledge the divinity of Jesus' (p 56). Revelation is truly a 'phallocentric text' (p 84).

This critique is hard to engage with, since Pippin does not state her methodology for interpreting the ethic of the text other than expressing her feminist convictions and laying out how Revelation fails to satisfy them. Pippin also deploys a curious 'flattening' of the text, so that the term 'apocalypse' is frequently used in the popular sense of 'cataclysmic crisis,' and any ambiguities, nuances or paradoxes in the text, even when noted, are subsequently ignored.[11] But Pippin does raise some important questions about gender, inclusivity and violence to which we shall return in the next chapter.

Allan Boesak: An Ethic of Resistance and Justification

Allan Boesak was a minister in the Dutch Reformed Mission Church of South Africa during the Apartheid era. He was for some time a leader in the black resistance to Apartheid rule, but was later involved in a financial scandal and discredited both as a religious and political leader.

His short commentary on selected chapters of Revelation, *Comfort and Protest*, makes fascinating reading, not least because (it is claimed in the introduction) it was born of an experience of an 'angelic visitation' that Boesak had whilst imprisoned in solitary confinement by the South African authorities. It was originally planned in 1980, at the height of the violence associated with protests against Apartheid, and published in 1987, a year after the Dutch Reformed Church declared that Apartheid could not be scripturally justified.

This is no theoretical treatise. Forged in the white heat of oppression and struggle, Boesak's writing constantly makes direct connections between the text of Revelation and the situation he sees unfolding around him in South Africa. And in part, this making of direct connections is central to his methodology. In the writings of John of Patmos, Boesak is reading the writings of a 'fellow pilgrim on the way of protest' (p 11). In fact, he suggests, this is probably the only way that Revelation can be read; it 'can only be understood by those who share a common experience and a common faith' (p 15).

Boesak's writing constantly makes direct connections between the text and the situation he sees unfolding around him in South Africa

As part of this conviction, there is in Boesak's work a repeated rejection of 'academic considerations' in favour of an instinctive identification between the author of Revelation and those suffering under oppression. 'We see and understand the events of history from the underside' and that is what matters. On the other hand, Boesak does draw on a range of academic studies of Revelation, and is indebted to them for historical critical information which is vital to his making connections with the text. He explicitly rejects futurist, preterist and church historical interpretations in favour of the contemporary historical—Revelation must be understood from within its own historical and cultural context[12] (p 28), but cannot be limited to this, since the nature of prophecy is that it will find its fulfilment in different ways at different times in history (p 29).

Radical Identification

The identification between text and world is unequivocal, striking and emotive. The South African government *is* the power of Satan at work in Boesak's world. The paradox of the defeated dragon still pursuing his quarry on the earth is precisely reflected in the actions of the regime's

> *Boesak's identification between text and world is unequivocal, striking and emotive*

Minister for Law and Order and of the army: 'instant barbed-wire fences falling out of the back of a truck like deadly vomit out of the mouth of the dragon [see Rev 12.15]' (p 91). The lamb who was slain of Revelation 5 is the one who identifies with and can speak to those who have suffered the atrocities that Boesak has witnessed (p 59). Black Christians dance around a police vehicle containing one of their number singing 'The power of Satan is broken, alleluia!' until the police, bewildered and confused, release him (p 62). And the call to faithful witness is expressed in the statement of black students to the South African government that there is something greater than holding on to life: 'You can only kill us' (p 83).

Two things are worth noting about this identification. The first is that, although Boesak's comments about the oppressed sound quite Marxist in places, within the commentary there is no suggestion that a prior ideological conviction shapes his reading of Revelation or brings a critique of Revelation to bear. Boesak appears to be quite content to have his priorities shaped by what he finds in the text. The second thing worth noting concerns the question of violence. Such a strong identification of the South African regime with Satan might appear to warrant the use of force of every kind against it. But this is not the logic of Revelation, and it is not the logic of Boesak's comments either. At every point he makes much of the fact that the oppressed are the victims of violence rather than the defeated in battle; he frequently uses the language of struggle, but this is a struggle of ideas and moral supremacy, not a struggle of force. The passive ethic of resistance in fact lends moral weight to the case of the oppressed.[13]

So Revelation offers an ethic of resistance and justification. It pours the fuel of hope on the fires of resistance to the oppressive regime, and lends justification to those on this side of the argument who believe their cause is right. That, at least, is what it does for Boesak and his fellows; there is little hint as to what it might mean for those living with less stark choices.

Wes Howard-Brook and Anthony Gwyther: An Ethic of Critical Engagement

Howard-Brook and Gwyther's book *Unveiling Empire: Reading Revelation Then and Now* is unusual in many respects. The authors live on different continents on opposite sides of the Pacific Ocean, and they wrote the book without ever meeting. But it is clear that to a great extent they share a common ethical outlook; both were involved, at different times, in pouring their own blood over a warship as a protest against militarism (p xxi). The book immediately sets out the ethical concerns they have as they approach Revelation. One author introduces himself as living on the 'outposts of empire' (p xix) and outlines a sociological comparison between Australia's cultural and economic relationship with America and first-century Asia Minor's relationship with Rome.

The authors believe (p 157) that the contrasting images of the two cities, (New) Jerusalem and Babylon, provide the 'master metaphor' for the whole book. This contrast has an overture in the messages to the churches, in the call to repent (of collusion with Babylon) and stand firm (in citizenship of the New Jerusalem). The contrast finds fuller explication in the body of the book, and a full expression of it

The authors believe that the contrasting images of the two cities provide a 'master metaphor' for the whole book

in the climax of chapter 21 with its explicit depiction of the New Jerusalem and its contrast with the description of Babylon in chapters 17 and 18. So the authors are able to find resources for ethical reflection across the whole range of material in Revelation.

'Come Out of Her'
In the light of this master metaphor, Howard-Brook and Gwyther see the ethical call as having its clearest expression in the pivotal command to 'come out of her' (Rev 18.4) (p 183f). This is the most explicit expression of what has been implicit elsewhere—an urgent clarion call to 'defect' from one city and live as inhabitants of the other. They explore the ethical content of this call in a number of different ways. In relation to the shape of the text of Revelation, they see how the visions of the two cities compare (p 160), how each relates to canonical prophecy (pp 172 and 186), and the different aspects of lament and celebration concerning the cities. But, very interestingly, they then go on to explore the ethical implications of the worship of God in contrast to the

worship of the beast. This is relatively unusual, in that commentators often struggle to find clear connections between Revelation 4 and 5 and the rest of the book other than as context-setting. Here, connections are not only found, but are seen as integral to the message of the book, and as undergirding an ethical outworking of that message.

The final stage of the authors' argument is to contextualize the ethic in their own situation as they perceive it. This is done through the filter of the claims of empire. In chapter 3 they have already looked at the relation between Christianity and Rome; in chapter 8 they contrast the claims of empire made by Rome and the Book of Revelation. In chapter 9 they then look at the 'imperial' claims made by global capitalism and see how the patterns of empire now correspond with patterns of empire then, and how Revelation's critique can be brought to bear. Global capital must be served by national governments (the beast from the land makes inhabitants of the earth worship the beast from the sea, Rev 13.12), global capital exploits the poor (the merchants of the earth were made rich by the harlot, Rev 18.11), and cities and countries compete for the patronage of global capital, just as the cities in Asia Minor competed for patronage from Rome.

This last chapter ends with practical suggestions of how we can 'come out of her' in the form of a dialogue between the authors. Curiously, the writer of the foreword comments that prophecy has ethical content, in that the hearer is invited to respond and change to avert coming judgment, whereas apocalyptic is quite different. 'In apocalyptic we are spectators to events, while in prophecy we are called to change what we foresee' (p xvi). The authors take a rather different line, perhaps one that is more faithful to Revelation's claim to be prophecy *as well as* apocalypse. The imperative in Revelation is not to avert judgment—that is already certain. But it is to refuse to collaborate with the systems that will be subject to judgment, and that in itself has ethical implications. Thus we need to engage critically and act prophetically—to live in a way that anticipates the empire to come.

Hal Lindsey: An Ethic of Suspicion and Crisis

Hal Lindsey's *The Late Great Planet Earth* was written at the end of the 1960s, published in 1970, and was reprinted 16 times within 18 months. It continues in print, in a revised edition, and the back cover of the latest edition claims that 'The New York Times called it the "no. 1 non-fiction bestseller of the decade"…The years since have confirmed Lindsey's insights into what biblical prophecy says about the times we live in.'

Lindsey's book is by no means a commentary on Revelation; he claims to be revealing the way in which biblical prophecies (mostly, as it happens, from the apocalyptic texts in Ezekiel, Daniel and Revelation) are about to be fulfilled in world events. However, key passages from Revelation form some of the most important elements of his scheme, and this scheme is then played back and used as a hermeneutical key for the reading of the whole of the book. But it is undoubtedly an ethical use of the text. The theological framework is more or less assumed; the texts in Revelation are used to evaluate events and issues in contemporary society, and adopt a practical stance in relation to them.

Lindsey sits firmly within the Dispensational school of thinking mentioned in chapter 1, and recent editions of the book are promoted alongside the 'Left Behind' series of novels which are set during the time of the Tribulation following the Rapture of Christians from the earth. Although nearly 35 years old, it still represents a way of reading apocalyptic texts, incorporating a form of Christian Zionism, which is probably more widespread now than it was when first published.

> *Lindsey claims that his approach to reading the Bible is literal, but it is not always clear what he means by this*

Lindsey claims that his approach to reading the Bible is literal (p 176). But it is not always clear what he means by this (he sometimes uses the term to mean 'by etymology'; see p 119 on Isaiah 47.5) and it is certainly clear that he does not read the text in this way, or in fact in any one consistent way. The use of *pharmakoi* meaning sorceries (in Rev 9.21 with cognates elsewhere) is really a criticism of Sixties student drug culture—largely because we get the English word 'pharmacy' from it (p 125).[14] Words can stand for other things that Lindsey deduces from his own arguments. 'Wherever you see the word "Chaldean" it can be translated equally well as "astrology"' (p 121). And they can be adapted to have relevance within his political scenario; the chariots of Dan 11.40 are mechanized infantry (p 154), and the locusts of Rev 9.2–11 are clearly helicopters. Yet at other times Lindsey is content to treat things like the four horsemen as 'figures' or metaphors (p 153). But at times the text is treated quite carelessly. The ten horns, Lindsey tells us, are ten nations of the European union (p 105), despite 17.12 telling us that they stand for ten kings. And the great harlot is a 'religious system' tied in with the return of the Antichrist (p 104), despite 17.18 telling us that it is 'the great city that rules over the king of the earth.'[15]

Biblical Hopscotch?

This flexible use of the text allows him to take different parts of Revelation[16]and other parts of the Bible and build them together into his picture of what the future holds.[17] In ethical terms, the picture looks in many ways like a

> *In ethical terms, the picture looks in many ways like a defence of the American way of life*

defence of the American way of life, perhaps especially defined from Middle America.[18] Lindsey is not afraid to deploy the starkest generalizations—the Chinese are the 'Yellow Peril' (the title of chapter 7) or 'Red China.' 'Liberals' are all clearly a Bad Thing. And Communism it undoubtedly the enemy; Europe will lose confidence in America because its anti-Communist commitment is not strong enough (p 95). But this is pro-Americanism with a difference. Lindsey confidently predicts that American power will be eclipsed by Europe (p 96), because according to his scheme (so detailed he even includes charts showing where the Russian amphibious assault will land) it has no place in the biblical prophecies about the end times. This is probably not a surprise for texts from a time when the continent was unknown.

Alongside this is an ethic of suspicion. If someone, somewhere has suggested something that might possibly be the case, and this fits with Lindsey's scheme, it is probably going to happen. There are numerous unattributed or untraceable quotations throughout the book. But perhaps the most remarkable thing about the whole book's ethic is that Lindsey asks us to do—precisely nothing! The last three pages of the book tell us what is needed. The main thing is to make sure we are on the right side—to open the door of our hearts (Rev 3.20). But other than that, the main thing is to 'look' and passively watch the plan of history unfold before our eyes. Revelation here is a prophetic cinematic experience; take your seat, and enjoy the show until you reach the final curtain.

Revelation here is a prophetic cinematic experience; take your seat, and enjoy the show until you reach the final curtain

3

Four Hot Potatoes

Given such a range of ways in which Revelation is read for ethics, is it possible to talk about the ethics of Revelation in any meaningful way—without simply side-stepping into a debate about hermeneutics?

If the process of reading is viciously circular, so that one's assumptions about the text inevitably dominate the shape of one's reading, then probably not. However, if we believe that the text is not simply at the mercy of the reader, and is able to confirm certain readings and resist others, then it might well be possible to see the shape of the ethics of Revelation by looking at the way the text responds to different ethical readings. In the end, the only way we can assess the way a text is read or used is by going back to the data of the text itself. So in this section we will look at four key ethical issues—gender, violence, heterophobia (fear of the 'other') and politics—to see if the text either allows or resists some of the readings that have been proposed.

Gender

Is Revelation oppressive of women? There are two main answers given to this question within feminist criticism of the book. The most radical (that of Pippin) is 'Yes—and irredeemably so.' Revelation is so deeply and thoroughly misogynist that there is nothing that can be redeemed from it by any acceptable reading strategy, and Revelation's influence throughout history has been to be at the front of the church's historical oppression of women. A second answer (given by commentators like Schüssler Fiorenza and Yarbro Collins) is 'Yes—but a right reading strategy can redeem from the text something of value.' The reading strategy in question is usually to situate Revelation in its social and historical context. Even though there are many specific aspects of this which are much debated (including the fairly foundational question of whether the rhetoric of Revelation is responding to a context of actual persecution or not), there are broad matters of context that can account for the apparently misogynist language. What we need to seek is the deeper, more pervasive message of the book, which is one of justice and judgment, and allow that to take priority over the surface misogyny.

There are some wider questions concerning a feminist critique of the text that are beyond the scope of this booklet.[19] But there are some specific elements of feminist critiques which it is possible to respond to. Objections to the use of images of women in Revelation are that the images focus on sexual immorality, that the women are passive, and that they meet violent ends, thus producing a toxic nexus between dominance, death and desire (hence the title of Pippin's book).

The images concerned are those of Jezebel (in the message to Thyatira, Rev 2.20–24), the woman clothed with the sun in Rev 12, and the harlot (RSV, 'prostitute' in NIV and other modern versions) of chapter 17, along with the description of the New Jerusalem in chapter 21 as the bride. Jezebel is a prophetess who is teaching immorality (*porneuo*) and committing adultery (*moicheuo*) with members of the church. The woman clothed with the sun mostly has things done to her, and is taken to the desert for 1,260 days (or three and a half years) and then we lose sight of her in the narrative. The harlot who is the city that rules over the kings of the earth (17.18) has committed fornication (*porneuo*) with them, and in the end is stripped, eaten and burned by the ten horns and the beast (17.16).

At face value these are indeed gruesome images. But reading them is complex, and it is important to note some significant aspects of the way they are presented that are too often neglected.

- The dominant term for the despicable activity of Jezebel and the harlot is *porneuo*, translated 'to commit immorality' in RSV. But this term is always juxtaposed with terms suggesting wrong *spiritual* allegiances rather than wrong *sexual* ones. So the citing of Jezebel's immorality comes between citation of her being a false prophetess and teacher and leading people to eat food sacrificed to idols (2.20). The use of the term 'immorality' in the following verse as a catch-all further emphasizes the close relation between these terms.

- 17.2 talks of the 'wine of [the harlot's] fornication' on which the inhabitants of the earth have become drunk, whilst 17.6 talks of the harlot herself being 'drunk with the blood of the saints.' The Semitism 'wine of her fornication' should be understood to mean 'the wine which is her fornication.' In other words, sexual imagery and drunkenness are being deployed to describe wrong spiritual allegiances.

- Whilst there is plenty of material in Revelation that refers directly to sexual morality, all this suggests that much of the language associated with these two images stands in the Old Testament tradition of using the language of sexual allegiance as a metaphor for spiritual allegiance to Yahweh or other gods.

- On closer reading, the judgment of these two figures is also much less voyeuristic and gleeful than suggested. The end of Jezebel is not made explicit; the destruction of the harlot is (somewhat paradoxically) at the hands of horns and beast (17.16). In the extended celebration of the destruction of the harlot/city in chapter 18 that follows, the metaphor of the harlot actually disappears from view; all the language of desolation and smoke and trade ceasing belong firmly to a description of Babylon as a city.

- The woman of chapter 12 is left in the desert and disappears from view—as in fact do others in the drama. The two witnesses of Rev 11 likewise do not reappear later in the drama. This is not a function of the particular images, but is a function of Revelation's episodic nature, probably due to its drawing on a wide range of influences.[20]

- For many of the female images, there are male counterparts. Other than Jezebel, the messages to the churches mention by name 'the Nicolaitans,' (2.6, 15)[21] 'the teaching of Balaam' (2.14) and Satan/the devil—all negative, masculine images. And the saints in general appear mostly passive, and 'done to,' being martyred in chapter 6 and trampled by the beast in chapter 13.

- The general emphasis on passivity has led to a strong strand of 'quietist' interpretation of Revelation, and makes Pippin comment (p 47) that both male and female are silenced and destroyed. This does make it difficult to defend the view that this is the misogynist fate of the female figures only.

The highly metaphorical nature of the images, both male and female, does raise the question about the relation of this text to subsequent readings of it. Can these images be read 'just' as metaphors, without carry-over of meaning onto the vehicles of the metaphors, that is, into a literal reading? For example,

To press her accusation of misogyny, Pippin has to adopt a peculiarly literal reading of Revelation

is it possible to read language of the death of the great harlot simply as a metaphor for the destruction of Roman Imperial power, without it expressing hatred of women?

The simple answer from observing the way metaphor works is 'yes.' Metaphors have an extraordinary way of establishing their own semantic ranges, quite separate from the literal semantic range. To press her accusation of misogyny, Pippin has to adopt a peculiarly literal reading of Revelation (so the kings of the earth entering the New Jerusalem in Rev 21 is an image of mass intercourse, since the city is the bride) and she supports her reading with the use of imagery (rather than commentary) since visual representations of the text are always literalizing.[22]

The text actually resists the kind of misogynist readings that some feminist critiques suggest are inevitable

So the interweaving of metaphorical imagery and the wider ambiguity about gender stereotypes means that the text actually resists the kind of misogynist readings that some feminist critiques suggest are inevitable.

Violence

Is Revelation a violent text? There are certainly plenty of violent images—devastation of the earth, rocks falling on people, burning lakes and eating of flesh. At the climax of the book, the images of judgment seem all the sharper because of their juxtaposition with the images of bliss. But as with the language of gender, the language of violence in Revelation is more nuanced than certain readings allow. The key questions are: Does Revelation depict a violent world? Does Revelation lead to a violent response? And does Revelation portray a violent God?

In answering these questions, we need to consider a number of factors.

- We have just left what many would argue has been the most violent century of world history (in terms of the number killed or injured by war). And yet many reading Revelation from a Western perspective come with a highly ambiguous view of violence. Most of us have little experience of violence first hand, and are shocked when we encounter it in person. And yet we are over-familiar with violence second-hand through the media—whether as reporting of real violence in other places, or as part of 'entertainment' on television and in film. As a result, responses of Western readers to violence in texts are often polarized; some readers are completely indifferent, whilst others can only respond with revulsion.

- The violence we are presented with in Revelation is a literary phenomenon, rather than being visual, and is presented in a highly stylized manner—one quarter or one third of the world is devastated, unimaginably large armies are on the march, birds feast on flesh in brutal but brief descriptions. This means that, unlike with visual media, we always have the option to read these texts more or less literally. And the literary interconnectedness of the text means that any of these individual episodes will need to be read in the light of the wider structure and movement of the book, as well as in its canonical context (that is, its place within Scripture as a whole).

- Thus we need to recognize that certain reading strategies are more problematic than others in presenting Revelation's violent imagery. A futurist approach, which sees Revelation more or less as a prediction of events to come in the 'end times' (understood chronologically as the last few years in history before Christ's return, rather than theologically as the era of the outpouring of the Spirit as in Joel 2/Acts 2) and adopts a literalizing reading, presents to us the images in Revelation as future, literal and intentional acts of God. On the other hand, a 'contemporary historical' reading, which wishes properly to locate the text in its historical context, will see Rev 12 as a description of the significance of Christ's life, ministry and death. And so it will read the series of seals and trumpets as a depiction of judgment made known *through the way the world already is*. This moves the problem of violence in Revelation into the wider context of the problem of evil in the world.

- A key issue in reading the violence in the text concerns our response to it. If we are removed in our own lives from experiences of violent oppression, then the experience of reading about the violent judgment of oppressors can simply be voyeuristic. However, for those subject to oppression (real or imagined), reading about the 'destruction of the destroyers' (Caird's comment on Rev 19.17, recalling Rev 11.18)[23] can be both a cathartic and empowering experience.

- A degree of detachment from the immediate impact of the violence can allow us to read the text carefully, and see more clearly the shape of Revelation's depictions of violence and judgment. A consistent theme of Revelation is the inherent (self) destructiveness of evil—hence the destruction of the city/harlot by the beast and horns itself at the end of Revelation 18, and the association of the beast and Satan with the Abyss in Rev 9.2 and 11 and Rev 20.1–3.

- A vital part of any reading is to note the reluctance of the text to associate the one seated on the throne directly with acts of judgment. As Richard Bauckham notes, it is the living creatures who belong to God's throne (4.6) that commission the judgments, and angels carry them out (6.1, 3, 5, 7, 15.7).[24] At the end of the judgments, the great voice which declares their completion is not directly attributed to the one on the throne but is simply said to come 'from the throne' (16.17). This kind of indirectness follows Jewish practice of avoiding any kind of anthropomorphism in describing God, and is part of Revelation's careful depiction of both God's transcendence and his sovereignty. And the lack of anthropomorphism undercuts accusations that Revelation is simply projecting images of human despotism onto heaven. However, in sharp contrast the end of the vision abandons any such reticence; in the New Jerusalem, God is present with his people to comfort them in person (21.4). Hesitation in associating God with judgement gives way to certainty that his presence means comfort and an end to all sorrow and pain.

Steve Moyise explores the apparent contradiction between the images of Jesus as the lamb who was slain, and the lion of the tribe of Judah conquering his foes. Should the image of conquering be interpreted through (and therefore modified by) the image of the sacrificial lamb—or should the image of the lamb be interpreted through the image of the conquering victor?[25] Moyise contrasts those who believe the first, and thus see the imagery of Christ and his judgment as acceptable, with those who do the second, and so find the imagery of judgment unacceptable, since Christ meets violence with violence and abuse with abuse.

Moyise seeks to resolve the dilemma by arguing for a postmodern, reader-centred approach to the text, where the reader can choose which of these motifs to 'foreground' and make primary. But he also acknowledges that it is not simply a case of 'either/or.' The two images in fact interpret each other, and need to be kept in tension, allowing no simple resolution.

The two images in fact interpret each other, and need to be kept in tension, allowing no simple resolution

Does the text then sanction the use of violence? Certain reading strategies may make readers passive in the face of violence. On the one hand, as Boesak hints, there is a tradition of passive resistance in response to the book, taking up the opening theme that patient endurance is the mark of those who in Jesus share both kingdom and suffering (Rev 1.9). On the other hand, the inevitability of the images of judgment may desensitize readers to possibilities of violence in which they are implicated. The reporter Ann Mojtabai has documented the way dispensationalist reading of Revelation has allowed citizens of Amarillo, Texas to build nuclear warheads with a quiet conscience.[26]

The question of violence in relation to metaphorical texts of judgment is found *in nuce* in other places in Scripture, such as the injunction to be kind to one's enemy and so 'heap burning coals on [your enemy's] head.' Despite the obvious violence of the image, the effect (in the text and, in my experience, in life) is an ethic of boundary-crossing love.

Heterophobia

Heterophobia—fear of the 'other'—is a sometimes hidden but sustaining theme in many contemporary aspects of cultural and ideological clashes. 'Inclusivity' is often portrayed as the non-negotiable virtue, and exclusivity correspondingly the non-negotiable sin. As I write, Michael Howard, the leader of the Conservative opposition to Government, has just announced a proposed limitation on immigration to Great Britain. Any rational argument for such a measure is dogged by the possible association of the position with irrational fear and hatred of the 'other,' a gut reaction against the British way of life being threatened or eroded by a creeping growth of supposedly unBritish ideas and patterns of living.

The eschatological focus of the book sharpens differences and resolves grey into black and white

Within the Anglican Communion, in the debate about homosexuality there have been accusations of homophobia. But if there is irrational fear present, it should be more accurately described as heterophobia, fear of another way of life and another way of looking at the world. Whatever the rational merits of the 'traditional' side of the argument, some of the language used suggests that there are also irrational elements at work in some places.

Against all this, Revelation does not appear to fare too well. The eschatological focus of the book, where people, institutions and power structures are evaluated in terms of their destiny in God's final judgement, sharpens differences and resolves shades of grey into black and white. So those who oppose the faithful are demonized as a 'synagogue of Satan' (2.9), failure to listen to Revelation's message of the words of Jesus and the Spirit leads to dire consequences (2.5 and 3.16), and there is a litany of judgement of the groups who refuse to accept the book's warnings (9.21, 21.8).

Inhabitants, Nations and Kings of the Earth
Against this, Revelation presents a universality in its vision of salvation which is much less explicit in Old Testament texts on which it draws, and entirely absent from other contemporary apocalyptic literature which sees salvation as belonging to a small faithful remnant whilst the majority of humanity suffers judgement. We can see this by looking at words and phrases used in Revelation to describe the response of humanity to the acts of God.

The term 'inhabitants of the earth' occurs ten times, and appears at first reading to be entirely negative. This group is distinguished from God's people (3.10) and indeed are guilty of their blood (6.10) and the enemies of the two witnesses (11.10); they are deceived by the second beast (13.8, 14, 17.8), are drunk with the harlot's wine (17.2) and come under God's judgement (8.13, 13.8, 17.8). And yet even here there are hints of hope. The very similar phrase 'those who sit on the earth' in 14.6 describes those to whom the gospel is proclaimed, suggesting (in parallel with 9.20) that repentance is still a real possibility. John, having eaten the little scroll, is called to prophesy 'to many peoples' (Greek *epi*; better than NIV 'about'), a sharp contrast to the episode in Ezekiel to which this alludes, where, having eaten his scroll, the prophet is specifically commanded to go to the house of Israel and '*not* to many peoples' (Ez 3.6, emphasis mine).

This universal vision becomes clearer in relation to 'the nations' and 'the kings of the earth.' Whilst the nations appear to be aligned with the powers of evil and taken in by them (see, for example, 14.8, 18.3 and 23, 20.3 amongst the 15 occurrences of the phrase), their destiny is to worship God (15.4) and this comes to pass in the vision of the New Jerusalem, where 'the nations will walk by its light… the glory and honour of the nations will be brought into it' (21.24–26). Similarly, the 'kings of the earth' are consistently aligned with the beast and harlot, but they too will 'bring their splendour into' the city (21.24). Richard Bauckham comments on this:

> Does Revelation expect the nations to be won from satanic deception and converted to the worship of God, or does it expect them to persist in rebellion until they perish under God's final judgement? In which of these ways does 'the kingdom of the world' become 'the kingdom of our Lord and his Messiah' (11.15)? The evidence seems to point both ways and commentators seem unable to give equal weight to all of it. (*Climax of Prophecy*, p 242)

This ambiguity and the move towards a universal vision is even more evident in Revelation's use of the phrase 'every tribe and tongue and people and nation' and its variants—a fourfold phrase that occurs seven times (5.9, 7.9, 10.11, 11.9, 13.7, 14.6 and 17.15) though never in the same order.[27] The first occurrence, in 5.9, appears to be an allusion to Exodus 19.5, 'you shall be my treasured possession out of all peoples' but interprets it using the refrain 'families, languages, lands and nations' from Genesis 10.5, 20 and 31, the only four-fold description of the nations of the world in the Old Testament. The effect of this is to turn a statement that could be understood in ethnically exclusive terms into a statement of the international and ethnically inclusive nature of the people of God.

These considerations imply that the denunciation of groups, whether specified in the messages to the churches or identified later in Revelation, should be understood as denunciation of behaviours and those who insist on these behaviours as a rejection of the call to repent, rather than as in any sense ethnically exclusive. The charge of exclusivity, in this sense, could only be sustained by demonstrating that the behaviours in question were defined in an 'essentialist' rather than a 'constructivist' way, that is, that these behaviours were inseparable from the identity of those involved.[28]

This charge could only be sustained by demonstrating that these behaviours were inseparable from the identity of those involved

Politics

Revelation is often popularly read in a 'spiritualised' way, giving encouragement to the individual believer but not inviting engagement with political realities. Elsewhere in the New Testament, Romans 13 offers a positive theology of state power as an instrument of God and therefore invites or sanctions involvement in politics. By contrast, Rev 13 paints a negative picture of state power as the enemy of God and therefore something dangerous and to be avoided. And yet these two depictions of political power are not as far apart as they appear.

Revelation comes from a world which knows nothing of a separation of the 'religious' and the 'political' and its language of power reflects this more integrated perspective. In deploying the phrases 'Alpha and Omega,' 'the keys of death and Hades' and 'I am coming quickly,' Revelation is taking over claims to power from Graeco-Roman magic cults and ascribing this power to Jesus alone. Similarly, the vision of worship in Rev 4 pulls together images of power from both what we could call the 'religious' and the 'political' spheres and ascribes them to the one on the throne and to the lamb. Thrones, living creatures, lightning and thunder, rainbows and jewels all belong to the biblical theophany. But elders in white casting golden crowns and singing chants of praise belong unmistakably (at least to first-century ears) to the world of political power, to the obeisance done in the presence of the conquering emperor who claims to be the true source of peace and prosperity. (For details of both these examples, see B 28 *How to Read the Book of Revelation* chapter 3.)

In this sense, Revelation's vision is close to that of Romans 13 in seeing all power as belonging to God. Paul's expression of this might suggest an almost passive acceptance of state power, and has been used to justify all sorts of compromises between church and state. But Rev 13 offers a complementary picture of the struggle for control, and so invites a more radical engagement with issues of power in the political realm.

Metaphorical Ethics

4

Unlike other didactic material in the New Testament (and the Old), Revelation does not contain very much by way of ethical instruction.

Where it does contain instruction to readers, the commands are of a general nature: 'remember' (2.5); 'hear' (2.7 and elsewhere); 'be faithful' (2.10); and so on. There is little situated response to specific ethical challenges. This is a sharp contrast to, for example, the structure of the Pauline epistles, where a context-setting engagement with theology then leads to specific ethical instructions in relation to life in the body and in the wider community.[29]

There is little situated response to specific ethical challenges

Yet Revelation, as a letter itself (note the clear letter form in 1.4), is directed to a specific situation in first-century Asia Minor. How then does it embody ethical principles? The answer lies in the metaphorical nature of its language, and so we need to reflect on how metaphor works.[30] (Revelation is sometimes described as using 'symbolic' language or imagery, but these two terms refer to something outside of the world of texts. A lit candle may be a symbol of God's presence; to say 'God is light' is to coin a metaphor.)

The heart of metaphor involves bringing together things that are dissimilar, and making a connection of similarity between them. This is the case whether the coining of the metaphor is direct predication ('I am the bread of life'), takes the form of a simile ('I saw one looking like a son of man') or is implied ('the lamb was on the throne'). In each case, the explicit or implied *subject* (in each of these cases, 'I,' 'the one,' and the person 'the lamb' is standing for, Jesus) is brought together with the *vehicle* of the metaphor ('bread,' 'son of man,' 'lamb') in order to express the *tenor* of what the metaphor is saying. In these metaphors the tenor of each is, respectively, sustenance, humanity or vulnerability, and the sacrificial offering. But of course the moment we start discussing the tenor of the metaphor, we are getting into questions of the interpretation of metaphor, and this will require thinking about the original historical and literary context of the terms at the very least.

This understanding of metaphor has some significant implications.

- **The identification of subject and vehicle involves** *making a claim about the nature of reality.* To claim, for example, that Roman Imperial power is a beast from the sea bearing the authority of the serpent, the primeval opponent of God, is not mere rhetoric but is a radical assertion about the true origin and identity of this political power. It is a claim that goes against the Empire's own ideal and against the view of the majority, and in this sense creates (in those who accept this claim) a 'cognitive minority,' a group whose conceptual world has a different shape from that of the majority.

- **This metaphorical predication is** *partial* **and so** *open to reapplication* **in new contexts.** Unlike in a literal predication, where the subject and the predicate are fully identified, in a metaphorical predication only some aspects of the subject of the metaphor are like some aspects of the vehicle of the metaphor. Even though my friend eats like a horse, I still set cutlery (not a nosebag) when he comes round for dinner! In coining the metaphor, certain elements of the subject are shorn off; historical details and particulars disappear from view, and we are left with the essential aspects of the subject expressed in the vehicle. And the literary context often indicates the essentials that are left. So, in Rev 13, the beast from the sea is concerned with self-promotion, with image, with economic control, and with oppression of the saints. In this sense, the metaphorical process is one step away from caricature, and in a visual medium we see the same kind of thing happening in political cartoons.[31] This removal of particularities, this caricaturing, is what makes the text open to reapplication in different contexts—in this case, wherever a political, religious or economic regime becomes obsessed with self-promotion, financial control, image and opposition to God's people it begins to look rather beast-like.

- **This claim about reality actually effects an open-ended** *reconfiguration of the perceived world.* Every metaphorical predication involves not just making claims about the subject of the metaphor, but about the vehicle and indeed the way spheres of reality are related to one another. To say that God is a compassionate father (Ps 103.13) not only changes our perception of who God is, it also changes our perception of what fatherhood is—a potential reflection of the divine. And suddenly, two whole spheres of human experience, worship of God and family relations, become interlinked. Likewise, to claim that Roman Imperial power is not the bringer of peace and prosperity but the latest manifestation of the chaos monster of old, brings together two areas of perception into a powerful, integrated view of reality. And it is in this reconfiguration that Revelation has its ethical power. Rather than offer direct ethical instruction, what the text says to us is: 'Accept this way of seeing the world—and act accordingly.'

So perhaps Revelation is not so much offering us an ethic for living in our world, but offering a paradigm by which we might develop an ethic for our own context. Revelation re-works Daniel's numerology of the period of tribulation ('time, times and half a time' Dan 12.7, Rev 11.11 and elsewhere) as 1,260 days (11.3, 12.6, instead of Daniel's 1,290 or 1,335) so that we are all, until the coming of the New Jerusalem, in the overlap of the ages, subject to the trampling of the beast but also benefiting from the protection of the desert.[32] So we too, just like the author of Revelation and its first readers, need to re-imagine our world in biblical terms—reconfiguring reality using biblical metaphors—and then act accordingly.

Thus we can see both how Revelation might offer quite a different ethic for Christians living in different situations and contexts. In a context where the patterns of power have historically been substantially shaped by a biblical ethic, the discernment of 'beastliness' may be quite a different task compared with that same task in a context where this has never happened. But Revelation's radical re-imagining—and the examples of its redeployment above—warns us against simplistic or complacent readings.

In redeploying these metaphors we will have to make decisions which depend on the way we perceive our world

Moreover, the embedding of its ethic in the metaphorical reconfiguration shows why the discernment of Revelation's ethics is inextricably linked with hermeneutics. Metaphor itself offers a hermeneutic of its own world; the coining of metaphor involves evaluation and selectivity. In redeploying Revelation's metaphors we will have to make decisions about where we see a correspondence of relations between our world and the world of the text, and this will depend on the way we already perceive our world.

Revelation and the Ethical Task

Finally, it is worth reflecting on how the way in which Revelation presents its vision lays down some challenges to the task of developing an ethic for living in the world.

There are three distinctive aspects to how Revelation presents itself which I believe are especially pertinent here. In the first place it claims to be a revelation (*apokalypsis* Rev 1.1); this term, occurring uniquely here amongst apocalyptic literature gives the whole genre its name. Secondly, it is thoroughly eschatological in its outlook; the whole of its ethical engagement with its world is predicated on the eschatological destiny of the two alternative cities of Babylon and Jerusalem. Indeed, there have been times when the word 'apocalyptic' has simply been taken to mean 'eschatological.' Thirdly, Revelation is the most explicitly Trinitarian book of the New Testament, and has a particular focus on the cosmic role of the Spirit. As the risen Jesus addresses the Christian communities, it is the Spirit who makes his voice heard (chapters 2 and 3). The seven eyes of the lamb are the Spirit roaming around the world, seeing what is happening. And at the end of the book, it is the Spirit with the Christian community who longs for the advent of the one who is to come. Each of these three aspects of the book challenges certain approaches to the ethical task.

- *Revelation.* The perspective of the book is rooted in the revelatory act of God. There is a presumption here that the true nature of things cannot be discerned and so right ethical decisions cannot be made without supernatural revelation. This might offer a challenge to ethical systems that are primarily rooted in natural theology, and might even challenge utilitarian ethical systems, which presume to know what really is of utility or of ultimate good for human beings.

- *Eschatology.* There is a presumption that it is destiny and the future which determines the ethical importance of certain stances. Although the certainty of judgment presented in Revelation distinguishes it from the majority of prophetic texts in the Bible, its call for a kind of prophetic faithfulness to the testimony of Jesus as witness to the coming of the New Jerusalem makes it closely allied with a concept of a 'prophetic' ethic. This might challenge a consequentialist ethic which limits its calculations to the visible impact of actions alone, as well as challenging any situational ethic which takes a short-term view of the context of action. In this sense, Revelation may offer something akin to a virtue ethic; in the light of what is to come, certain actions or dispositions are virtuous in and of themselves.

- *Pneumatology.* Finally, there is a presumption that the work of the Spirit, the 'seven eyes of the lamb that roam the earth,' is indispensable to right action, both in terms of discernment and empowering. This argues against a rationalistic approach to ethical decision-making and suggests that ethics cannot be divorced from discipleship—the ethical task involves more than mere clear thinking and good education.

Notes

1   A full transcript of the film's dialogue can be found at http://corky.net/scripts/apoca-lypseNow.html. (checked January 2005).

2   Scholarly questioning of whether Revelation was responding to a perceived crisis or actu-ally trying to create such a crisis was in modern times pioneered by Leonard Thompson, *The Book of Revelation: Apocalypse and Empire.* (Oxford: OUP, 1990).

3   There is an excellent overview of the development and growth in popularity of dispen-sationalism in chapter 1 of Wes Howard-Brook and Anthony Gwyther, *Unveiling Empire* (New York: Orbis, 1999).

4   For a brief but very helpful exposition of the different views of the millennium see Michael Gilbertson *The Meaning of the Millennium* (Grove Biblical booklet B 5). See also the tabular summary on the Grove resources page supporting B 28 *How to Read the Book of Revelation* at www.grovebooks.co.uk

5   This is the assumed backdrop behind the 'Left Behind' series by Tim LaHaye, sub-titled 'Tribulation Force.' For an outline of the interpretative problems with this reading, see 'The Use and Abuse of Revelation' by Ian Paul, *The Bible in Transmission* July 2003, avail-able at the online resources pages for this booklet at www.grovebooks.co.uk For an online critique of dispensationalism, see http://users.frii.com/gosplow/disp2.html

6   For details see Ian Paul, *How to Read the Book of Revelation* (Grove Biblical booklet B 28) pp 22–24.

7   There is, for example, a widespread consensus that the Revised Common Lectionary continues to under-represent Revelation in its scheme of readings. For criticism of this in the Church of England's General Synod, see the proceedings at http://www.cofe.anglican.org/about/gensynod/proceedings/ especially July 2004.

8   For details of the way in which genre changes in Revelation and some of the implications, see B 28 *How to Read the Book of Revelation* Chapter 2.

9   On the use of the term 'futurist' see B 5 *The Meaning of the Millennium*, B 28 *How to Read the Book of Revelation*, or the web pages supporting B 28 at www.grovebooks.co.uk

10   Louisville: Westminster/John Knox, 1992.

11   For example, the quotation from p 47 cited above follows immediately on from Pip-pin noting that, in fact, both male *and* female figures in Revelation are silenced and destroyed—this is not something reserved for the female. But this datum does not then feature in her ideological evaluation of the text.

12   This is something that Pippin explicitly rejects, in contrast to her feminist predecessors Yarbro Collins and Schüssler Fiorenza.

13   I believe that there were times when Boesak was ambiguous as to whether resistance by force was justified—but there is no hint of this in the commentary.

14   Commentators universally maintain that this should be translated 'sorceries' because of the context in Revelation and the significance of the term in OT texts to which Revelation alludes. See, for example, David Aune, *Revelation* (Word, Waco: 1999) p 544.

15   Lindsey later tells us that in fact the harlot is both these things.

16   His use of Revelation is so out of order that it is quite difficult at times to follow the logic of his interpretation, or to understand his overall scheme for the book until the end.

17   Lindsey does admit that this hopping from one place to another might look to some like 'biblical hopscotch' were it not for the fact that his conclusion is so coherent (p 119).

18   On this, William Stringfellow, *An Ethic for Christians and Other Aliens in a Strange Land* (Waco: Word, 1973) p 13 comments: 'The task is to treat the nation within the tradition of

biblical politics—to understand America biblically—*not* the other way around, *not* (to put it in an appropriately awkward way) to construe the Bible Americanly.'

19 To what extent is such an 'ideological critique' a reasonable reading strategy? Should not the critique run both ways—the text critiquing the ideology as well as the other way around? Where do we find a definition of what constitutes 'liberation' for women (or any group, come to that) by which we judge whether Revelation is liberating or oppressive? Is there coherence in a reading strategy that strongly excludes another reading strategy—on the grounds that the strategy in question is itself exclusive?

20 It is this feature of the text which, on the one hand, means that it deploys a sometimes bewildering range of micro-genres. On the other, I believe that it is this which has given rise to (erroneous) theories of multiple written sources, such as that proposed some time ago by R H Charles and more recently by David Aune. It also presents us with specific exegetical challenges, such as how the millennium of chapter 20 fits in with the wider numerological schemes (on which see my B 28 *How to Read the Book of Revelation*).

21 This term appears to be derivative from the name Nicolaus (etymologically, 'conqueror of [the] people') but it is far from clear that it refers to an actual social grouping in the churches, as opposed to being a literary construct for rhetorical purposes.

22 We have recently experienced an interesting parallel to this. Our eldest daughter has become interested in the Harry Potter books, and has enjoyed reading them. But watching the films has unsettled her; the ideas become much more concrete and the metaphorical overtones of aspects of the books are lost.

23 G B Caird, *The Revelation of St John the Divine* (Black's, 1966) p 247. It is worth noting that Caird lived through the 2nd War, and explicity cites his reaction to evil powers as seen in it as an influence shaping his study of NT 'principalities and powers.'

24 Richard Bauckham, *The Theology of the Book of Revelation* (Cambridge: CUP, 1993) p 42.

25 'Does the lion lie down with the lamb?' in Steve Moyise (ed), *Studies in the Book of Revelation* (T and T Clark, 2001), available as a pdf to download from http://www.ucc.ac.uk/theology/PDF/Lion.pdf

26 There are some specific injunctions in the messages to the communities in chapters 2 and 3, but these focus on commendable qualities, such as being hard-working and perservering (Rev 2.2), having courage in the face of suffering (Rev 2.10) and so on. This is very different from specifying, for example, how to order marriage relationships, or from commending the obedience of slaves to masters, that we find in the 'household codes' in the Pauline and other epistles. The injunctions at the end of Revelation such as 21.8, appear to have an ideological purpose rather than an ethical imperative, identifying a group whose behaviours put them under judgement.

27 For a full discussion of this term, see Bauckham *The Climax of Prophecy* pp 326–337.

28 A further important consideration in assessing the language of the messages in Rev 2 and 3 in particular is the difference between inner-group expressions of hatred and intra-group expressions of disagreement. For a helpful exploration of this, see Steve Motyer *Antisemitism and the New Testament* (Grove Biblical booklet B 23) especially page 10.

29 A G Mojtabai, *Blessed Assurance* (Syracuse: Syracuse University Press, 1987)

30 In my explanation of metaphor I broadly follow the understanding developed by Paul Ricoeur, but with my own adaptations. For a fuller reflection on the interpretation of metaphor, see my article in the forthcoming *Baker Dictionary of Biblical Interpretation*, also available on the Grove web site supporting this booklet www.grovebooks.co.uk

31 For a collection of cartoons that follow exactly this pattern, see the supporting page on the Grove web site.

32 For an overview of the numerology, see B 28 *How to Read The Book of Revelation* chapter 6. For detail on Revelation's reworking of Daniel's numbers see Richard Bauckham, *The Climax of Prophecy* (T and T Clark, 1993) chapter 11, especially pages 401f.